The Shack: Unauthorized Theological Critique

Tim Challies

NIMBLE BOOKS LLC

ISBN-13: 978-1-934840-49-8

ISBN-10: 1-934840-49-1

Copyright 2008 Tim Challies

Version 1.0; last saved 2008-07-11.

Nimble Books LLC

1521 Martha Avenue

Ann Arbor, MI 48103-5333
http://www.nimblebooks.com

This book was produced using Microsoft Word 2007 and Adobe Acrobat 8.1. The cover was produced using The Gimp. The cover font, heading fonts and the body text inside the book are in Constantia, designed by John Hudson for Microsoft.

This book is an unauthorized theological and literary critique of the novel *The Shack* by William P. Young.

BOOK DESCRIPTION

In this booklet I hope to guide you through *The Shack*. We will look at the book with a charitable but critical eye, attempting to understand what it teaches and how it can be that opinions about the book vary so widely. We do this not simply to be critical, but as an exercise in discernment and critical thinking. We will simply look at what the author teaches and compare that to the Bible.

ABOUT THE AUTHOR

Tim Challies is a leading evangelical blogger, author of *The Discipline of Spiritual Discernment* and editor of Discerning Reader (www.discerning reader.com), a site dedicated to discerning reviews of books that are of interest to Christians. His daily commentary is available at www.challies.com. A self-employed web designer, Tim lives in the outskirts of Toronto, Ontario with his wife and three young children.

A READER'S REVIEW OF
THE SHACK

Introducing *The Shack*

The Shack is the unlikeliest of success stories. The first and only book written by a salesman from Oregon, it was never supposed to be published. William P. Young wrote the tale for the benefit of his children and after its completion in 2005, it was copied and bound at Kinko's in time for him to give it to his children for Christmas.

Shortly after he completed the book, Young showed the manuscript to Wayne Jacobsen, a former pastor who had begun a small publishing company. After the manuscript was rejected by other publishers, Jacobsen and his co-publisher Brad Cummings decided to publish it themselves under the banner of Windblown Media.

(continued on page 2)

contents

The three men, with only a $300 marketing budget at their disposal, began a word-of-mouth campaign to let people know about the book. The rest, as they say, is history.

Since its first publication *The Shack* has gone through printing after printing. There are now over a million copies of the book in print and its popularity continues to rise. The book has climbed as high as #8 on the USA Today bestseller list and at least as high among all books at Amazon.com where it is also approaching 500 reader reviews. Windblown Media is negotiating with film studios about the possibility of a movie version of *The Shack*. The publisher has also recently signed a distribution agreement with Hachette Books, which has now begun to handle sales, marketing, distribution, licensing, and manufacturing. The book is set to go even further and climb even higher in the months and years to come.

The Shack has been received among Christians with decidedly mixed reviews. While many have acclaimed it as a groundbreaking story that brings to life heart-stirring theology, others insist that some of what it teaches is patently unbiblical. Where Eugene Peterson, Professor Emeritus of Spiritual Theology at Regent College in Vancouver says it "has the potential to do for our generation what John Bunyan's *The Pilgrim Progress* did for his," Dr. Albert Mohler, President of Southern Baptist Theological Seminary says, "This book includes undiluted heresy." While singer and songwriter Michael W. Smith says "*The Shack* will leave you craving for the presence of God," Mark Driscoll, Pastor of Mars Hill Church in Seattle says, "Regarding the Trinity, it's actually heretical."

In this booklet I hope to guide you through *The Shack*. We will look at the book with a charitable but critical eye, attempting to understand what it teaches and how it can be that opinions about the book vary so widely. We do this not simply to be critical, but as an exercise in discernment and critical thinking. We will

> "People are not necessarily concerned with how orthodox the theology is. People are into the story and how the book strikes them emotionally..."
>
> (Lynn Garrett, Senior Religion Editor for *Publishers Weekly*)

simply look at what the author teaches and compare that to the Bible.

If you have not yet read the book, you may wish to read a short summary of it on the next page. Those who have already read it will probably wish to skip directly to page four.

Let's enter *The Shack* together!

VOCABULARY: TRINITY

"The doctrine of the Trinity affirms that God's whole and undivided essence belongs equally, eternally, simultaneously, and fully to each of the three distinct Persons of the Godhead."

Bruce Ware

THE SHACK IN 500 WORDS (OR LESS)

The Shack is a book that seeks to provide answers to the always timely question "Where is God in a world so filled with unspeakable pain?". It is a tale that revolves around Mack (Mackenzie) Philips. Four years before the story begins, Mack's young daughter, Missy, was abducted during a family vacation. Though her body was never found, the police did find evidence in an abandoned shack to prove that she had been brutally murdered by a notorious serial killer who preyed on young girls. As the story begins, Mack, who has been living in the shadow of his *Great Sadness*, receives a note from God (known in this story as Papa). Papa invites Mack to return to this shack for a time together. Though uncertain of what to expect, Mack visits the scene of the crime and there experiences a weekend-long encounter with God, or, more properly, with the Godhead.

Each of the members of the Trinity is present and each appears in bodily form. Papa, whose actual name is Elousia (which is Greek for *tenderness*) appears in the form of a large, matronly African-American woman (though near the book's end, because Mack requires a father figure, she turns into a pony-tailed, grey-haired man). Jesus is a young to middle-aged man of Middle-Eastern descent while the Holy Spirit is played by Sarayu (Sanskrit for *air* or *wind*), a small, delicate and eclectic woman of Asian descent. Mack also meets for a time with Sophia, who, like Lady Wisdom in Proverbs, is the personification of God's wisdom.

The reader learns that Mack has been given this opportunity to meet with God so he could learn to deal with his *Great Sadness*--the overwhelming pain and anger resulting from the death of his daughter. There is very little action in *The Shack* and the bulk of the book is dialog. The majority of the dialog occurs as the members of the Trinity communicate with Mack, though occasionally the author offers glimpses into their unique relationships with one another.

As the weekend progresses Mack participates in lengthy and impactful discussions with each member of the Trinity. Topics range from the cross to the Trinity and from forgiveness to free will. He finds his understanding of God and his relationship with God radically and irrevocably altered. His faith is dismantled piece by piece and then put back together. As we might expect, he leaves the cabin a changed man.

"With every page, the complicated do's and don't that distort a relationship into a religion were washed away as I understood Father, Son, and Holy Ghost for the first time in my life."

(Patrick M. Roddy, Emmy Award Winning Producer of ABC News)

VOCABULARY: THEOLOGY

"Theology is the application of Scriptures to all areas of human life."

John Frame

FACT AND FICTION

The Shack is a fictional tale. Though the story's narrator is identified as "Willie" (referring to William Young, the book's author) never is the reader expected to believe that the story is real. Yet though *The Shack* is fiction, it is clearly intended to communicate theological truths. It is meant to impact the way the reader thinks about God, about love and about life. It is not a book that was written only to share a story, but to share theology.

Fiction has often been used to communicate important truths. In his endorsement for this book Eugene Peterson references John Bunyan's *The Pilgrim's Progress* which stands as perhaps the most obvious example of theological fiction. We might also point to the works of C.S. Lewis and especially to the words of Jesus Christ, who often used stories and parables to communicate truth.

Those who read reviews of this book will soon find that people are claiming it has changed their lives and changed their understanding of God. Despite the book's genre, it is clearly communicating to people on a deeply spiritual level. It is impacting the way people think of God. The book's narrator admits as much where, in the After Words he says, "I don't think there is one aspect of my life, especially my relationships, that hasn't been touched deeply and altered in ways that truly matter." Examining the reviews posted by readers at Amazon.com and elsewhere across the Internet will reveal how deep an impact this book is making. Because of the book's impact we must be willing to examine it not only as a story but also as a tool for communicating information about the character and the work of God. And that is just what we will do.

AMAZON READER REVIEWS

"The character of God in the book is from a point of view I never would have imagined, or thought of. But all the answers and conversations are right on. It really changes the way I view God, and the way I can relate with him. My relationship is so much deeper now."

"I truly believe that 'The Shack' has the potential to shake up and alter the entire Church. This book will seriously mess with your theology -- and you will be GLAD. Yeah, it's really that good."

"Wish I could take back all the years in seminary! The years the locusts ate???? Systematic theology was never this good. Shack will be read again and again. With relish. Shared with friends, family, and strangers. I can fly!"

"It has changed me or rather I should say that God has used this book to alter my thinking as to who He is and who I am in His eyes... one who is greatly loved by Him. I've discovered that He is quite fond of me and you."

"Never will I look at the Trinity in the same way again. ... I have entered the shack and I will never be the same."

"Honestly, I don't think that there is a book other than the Bible itself that has influenced the dimension of my love for my Father, Jesus, and Sarayu... The visual imagery that the author has been able to convey through the eyes of Mack will forever impact my visions of my Trinitarian guardians."

WHAT IS THEOLOGY (AND WHY DOES IT MATTER)?

The word theology is one that is undoubtedly not very popular today. It is a word that comes loaded with all kinds of baggage. This is unfortunate, though, because whether we like it or not, we are all theologians.

The word theology is derived from two little Greek words. The root "theos" means "God" and the suffix "-ology" comes from the Greek word for "speak." So when we use the word "theology" we mean "speaking of God" or as has become the more popular definition, "the study of God." That doesn't sound so bad, does it? Anyone who has thought about God or who has spoken about God has been engaged in theology.

Of course theology is not enough; it is a means rather than merely an end. We do not wish to only know about God, but also wish to show evidence that we

> *"This amazing story will challenge you to consider the person and the plan of God in more expansive terms than you may have ever dreamed."*
>
> (From David Gregory's endorsement of *The Shack*)

know Him. We give evidence of this in the way we live our lives. Often times those who say they do not like theology are those who have known people like Mack's father–a man who claimed to love God, but whose life showed little evidence of the transformation we'd expect from someone who had truly met with God. There are many people who claim to be Christians but who have separated theology from practice, knowledge of God from the practice of serving him. No Christian can deny that we are called by God to learn more about Him and to study His ways. The more we learn of God, the more we are able to live in a way that pleases Him.

Of course there is good theology and bad theology. Good theology is theology that is consistent with what the Bible teaches us; bad theology is theology that is different from what the Bible teaches or that is even in direct opposition to what the Bible teaches.

Though *The Shack* is not a textbook for theology, and though it may not appear on the outside to be theological, as long as it discusses the nature and the plan of God, it must be so. In this guide we will look at the theology of *The Shack*, stopping often to consider the book in relation to the Bible. Theology is not often a good or noble end in itself, so we will look to the theology as the means to a greater end-- letting that theology inform our lives. When we know God as He is, we can honor God in the way we live. And isn't that what we all want?

The way to avoid being like Mack's dad is not to avoid theology, but to love and to embrace and to pursue it. Those men and women who live most like Christ are not the ones who know the least about Him, but the ones who know Him best. We wish to be Christians who know God deeply and intimately. And to know Him in that way we turn first to the Bible.

VOCABULARY: THE WORD OF GOD

"The word of God is His powerful, authoritative, self-expression in which he comes personally to be with us."

John Frame

ENTERING THE SHACK

In this section of the guide we will look at The Shack *and examine some of the underlying ideas and theological concepts within it. We will use care and discernment, simply comparing what this book teaches to what we find in the Bible.*

Subversion: Undermining the Faith

We will soon turn to three key theological concepts and examine what *The Shack* has to say about each of them. The topics we will look at are revelation, salvation and the Trinity. Before we do so, though, I would like to address one particularly disturbing and underlying aspect of this book. As I read the book I saw that, from beginning to end, *The Shack* has a quietly subversive quality to it. The author very subtly criticizes many aspects of the church and contemporary Christianity before replacing the concepts he criticizes with new ones. He criticizes seminary education ("Mack struggled to keep up with [Papa], to make some sense of what was happening. None of his old seminary training was helping in the least" (91).), the Bible ("God's voice had been reduced

> *"Mack struggled to keep up with her, to make some sense of what was happening. None of his old seminary training was helping in the least."*

to paper, and even that paper had to be moderated and deciphered by the proper authorities and intellects" (65-66).), Sunday School ("This isn't Sunday School. This is a flying lesson" (98).), the church as a body ("You're talking about the church as this woman you're in love with; I'm pretty sure I haven't met her...She's not the place I go on Sundays" (177).), the church as

individuals ("For Mack these words were like a breath of fresh air! Simple. Not a bunch of exhausting work and long list of demands and not the sitting in endless meetings staring at the backs of people's heads, people he really didn't even know. Just sharing life" (178).), family devotions ("Images of family devotions from his childhood came spilling into his mind, not exactly good memories...He half expected Jesus to pull out a huge old King James Bible" (107).), theological certainty ("I have a great fondness for uncertainty [said Sarayu]" (203).), the word "Christian" as a descriptor ("Who said anything about being a Christian? I'm not a Christian [said Jesus]" (182).) and on and on. Perhaps this statement from page 119 serves as an apt description of many of the book's subtle undertones: "I will tell you that you're going to find this day a lot easier if you simply accept what is, instead of trying to fit it into your preconceived notions." Though we certainly do need to maintain some objectivity when we study Scripture, God has also told us many things with certainty and we need to cling tightly to these. Many preconceived notions are theologically sound and informed by biblical truth. The reader of *The Shack* must be careful that he does not simply accept "what is," at least as William Young describes it, without critical thinking and spiritual discernment.

Revelation: How Can We Know God?

There are few doctrines more important to settle than the doctrine of revelation. It is this doctrine that teaches us how God has chosen to reveal Himself to human beings. While every theistic religion teaches that God chooses to communicate with humans, they vary radically in the ways He does so. Christians are known as being a people of the book, people who cling to the Scripture as the revealed will of God. The Bible, we believe, is a unique gift given to us as an expression of God's love—as an expression of Himself. Not surprisingly, revelation is central to *The Shack*.

Christians hold to the belief that the Bible is the only infallible source of God's revelation to us. The Bible alone teaches all that is necessary for our salvation from sin and is the standard by which all Christian behavior must be measured. The best place to begin with understanding the Bible is to learn what is says about itself.

The Bible testifies to its own uniqueness and sufficiency. "All Scripture is breathed out by God and profitable for teaching, for reproof, for correction, and for training in righteousness, that the man of God may be competent, equipped for every good work" (2 Timothy 3:16,17). It testifies to its own perfection and power. "The law of the Lord is perfect, reviving the soul; the testimony of the Lord is sure, making wise the simple" (Psalm 19:7). It testifies to its own completeness. "I warn everyone who hears the words of the prophecy of this book: if anyone adds to them, God will add to him the plagues described in this book, and if anyone takes away from the words of the book of this prophecy, God will take away his share in the tree of life and in the holy city, which are described in this book" (Revelation 22:18,19).

Clearly the Bible demands for itself a place of prominence and preeminence. It demands that it be held as God's most important revelation to us, Some people believe, though, that the revelation given to us in the Bible needs to be supplemented or superseded by fresh revelation. This is especially a temptation in an age like ours where we tend to value what is new more than what is ancient. A question worth asking is this one: does *The Shack* point Christians to the unfailing standard of Scripture or does it point them to new and fresh revelation?

Ever since humans fell into sin, the history of God's communication with people has been a history of mediation. Mediation is a concept we encounter often today. We hear of sports contracts being settled by mediation; we hear of lawyers becoming involved in mediation between divorcing couples. These hint at mediation as we understand it from the Bible. In rejecting God's goodness and benevolence and in putting himself in place of God, our forefather Adam erected a barrier between himself and God. The close communion that had once existed was ruptured and destroyed. No longer would God come walking with humans in the cool of the day; no longer would He allow them to stay in His Garden. He forced them out and barred the way so they could not return. The very next passage of Scripture relates the first murder. Human history had taken a drastic,

> *"God's voice had been reduced to paper, and even that paper had to be moderated and deciphered by the proper authorities and intellects."*

horrifying turn for the worse. The lines of communication had been shattered.

From that time, God no longer allowed people to commune with Him in the same way. From that point on, man could no longer approach God as he had in the Garden. He had to approach God through a mediator. When we think of mediators we may think first of Moses, a man to whom God revealed Himself and a man whose task it was to then make the will of God known to the Israelites. After Moses was Joshua, and after Joshua were judges and prophets. There were priests to stand between God and man, offering to God sacrifices on behalf of the people and bestowing God's blessings and curses on His behalf. Always there were mediators, always there were people standing between God and man. Always people must have realized their inability to approach God as they were. Always they must have wondered, "how can we approach God directly?"

God's revelation to us is now mediated communication. We may long for im-mediate or unmediated communication, but today our sin stands between us and the Holy God. God has given his full and perfect and sufficient revelation in the Bible. It is in the Bible that God gives us the rule as to how we may know Him and how we may live in a way that honors Him. How will God reveal himself to us according to William Young? "You will learn to hear my thoughts in yours" (195), says Sarayu. "You might see me in a piece of art, or music, or silence, or through people, or in Creation, or in your joy and sorrow. My ability to communicate is limitless, living and transforming, and it will always be tuned to Papa's goodness and love. And you will hear and see me in the Bible in fresh ways. Just don't look for rules and principles; look for relationship—a way of coming to be with us" (198). He may reveal Himself savingly through stories that merely and loosely parallel the story of Jesus' sacrifice (185). Young consistently downplays Scripture at the expense of personal

THE PILGRIM'S PROGRESS

The front cover of *The Shack* bears an endorsement from author and scholar Eugene Peterson in which he favorably compares the book to *The Pilgrim's Progress*, saying "This book has the potential to do for our generation what John Bunyan's *Pilgrim's Progress* did for his. It's that good!"

The Pilgrim's Progress is the work of John Bunyan, an English writer and preacher. It has been translated into more languages than any other book in history. Besides the Bible, no other book has been as widely printed and distributed. *The Pilgrim's Progress*, considered the finest of all Christian allegories, was first published in 1678. Remarkably, it has never gone out of print.

In 1658 John Bunyan was indicted for preaching without a license and two years later was consigned to prison. Because he refused to desist from preaching, the sentence was extended to twelve years. It was during this long imprisonment that he wrote *The Pilgrim's Progress*.

As an allegory, *The Pilgrim's Progress* uses fictional characters and situations to point to a greater reality. The main character, Christian, is an allegory for the journey each Christian must make as he journeys through life. One of the greatest works of Christian fiction and theology, *The Pilgrim's Progress* is a must-read for any Christian.

Did you Know?
Charles Spurgeon, one of history's most highly-regarded Christian preachers, considered *The Pilgrim's Progress* essential reading and claimed to have read it over 100 times!

experience. What Young indicates in *The Shack* is that we must expect God to reveal Himself in unmediated ways. God will reveal Himself to us in the Scripture, but only as one way out of many. Nowhere is Scripture given the place of prominence or uniqueness that it demands of itself. But without the Scripture as our norm, as our rule, we are subject to every whim. Only when we maintain the superiority of the Bible can we measure all of our behavior and all of our beliefs against the perfect measure given to us by God.

Despite the Bible's testimony to its own unique qualities, the majority of *The Shack's* references to Scripture are negative in their tone. They do not affirm the Bible as God's perfect revelation to us, but instead focus on its abuse at the hands of those who profess Christ or on supposed old-fashioned notions about it. Early in the book, for example, the reader learns that Mack has a seminary education, but one that downplayed the means God uses to reveal Himself. "In seminary he had been taught that God had completely stopped any overt communication with moderns, preferring to have them only listen to and follow sacred Scripture, properly interpreted, of course. God's voice had been reduced to paper, and even that paper had to be moderated and deciphered by the proper authorities and intellects. It seemed that direct communication with God was something exclusively for the ancients and uncivilized, while educated Westerners' access to God was mediated and controlled by the intelligentsia. Nobody wanted God in a box, just in a book. Especially an expensive one bound in leather with gilt edges, or was that guilt edges" (65-66)? Yet nowhere would the Bible indicate that it is God's voice "reduced" to paper. Nowhere would the Bible downplay its own importance as written revelation. There is nothing reductionistic about the Bible or the fact that it is written revelation! We must not downplay the beauty, the power or the sufficiency of the Bible.

Salvation: What Has Christ Accomplished?

Though the cross is central to the Bible and central to the Christian faith, it appears only sparingly in *The Shack*. A person who is unfamiliar with the Christian faith will not be able to glean from this book a biblical understanding of what the cross was for and what Jesus' death accomplished. Nor will he understand how God saves us and what He saves us from.

The Bible is clear that the cross is the very apex of the Christian faith. It is on the cross that Jesus Christ paid the penalty for sin. On the cross Jesus took upon Himself the sin of those who were His children and there He faced the penalty for such sin. The penalty He faced was the just wrath of the Father—the punishment due to those who would turn their backs on the Creator. On the cross we see that great mystery of Jesus becoming sin and of being separated from His Father so He might satisfy the demands of justice. This is the gospel! This gospel message is one that requires a response of faith. In faith we believe this and by grace

VOCABULARY: REDEMPTION

"Christ's saving work viewed as an act of 'buying back' sinners out of their bondage to sin and Satan through the payment of a ransom."

Wayne Grudem

we receive all the benefits of what Christ accomplished on that cross.

The Shack offers only hints as to the importance of the cross and to its function within the faith. "Honey," says Papa, "you asked me what Jesus accomplished on the cross; so now listen to me carefully: through his death and resurrection, I am now fully reconciled to the world." "The whole world? You mean those who believe in you, right?" "The whole world, Mack. All I am telling you is that reconciliation is a two way street, and I have done my part, totally, completely, finally. It is not the nature of love to force a relationship but it is the nature of love to open the way." What then is the nature of this reconciliation? Young never tells us in any clear way. What is clear, though, is that the God of The Shack is not a God who could have punished His Son for the sins of others. After all, Papa says, "Regardless of what he felt at that moment, I never left him" (96). He is not a

> *"When we three spoke ourself into human existence as the Son of God, we became fully human. We also chose to embrace all the limitations that this entailed. Even though we have always been present in his created universe, we now became flesh and blood."*

God who could have poured out upon His Son His just wrath for sin. In fact, God does not need to punish sin at all, says Papa. "I don't need to punish people for sin. Sin is its own punishment, devouring from the inside. It's not my purpose to punish it; it's my joy to cure it" (120).

We might now ask, Who can be reconciled to God? What is necessary for those who would establish a relationship with God? "Those who love me come from every stream that exists. They were Buddhists or Mormons, Baptists or Muslims, Democrats, Republicans and many who don't vote or are not part of any Sunday morning or religious institutions" (182). Mack asks for clarification. "Does that mean...that all roads will lead to you?" "'Not at all,' smiled Jesus...'Most roads don't lead anywhere. What it does mean is that I will travel any road to find you'" (182). While these words cannot rightly be said to actually teach universalism, the view that all men will go to heaven, neither do they clearly deny it. Is Jesus the only way to be reconciled to God? The book is less than clear on this point. Jesus says to Mack, "I am the best way any human can relate to Papa or Sarayu." Jesus does not say, "I am the way, and the truth, and the life. No one comes to the Father except through me," as he does in John 14:6, but merely states that He is the best way.

We are left with an incomplete gospel; a gospel message that says little of sin and of justice. It is a gospel message that says nothing of how we may be saved from the sin that pollutes us.

The Shack also muddles the concept of redemption. Redemption, according to Young, is not something that happened once and for all on the cross. Rather, he claims that God has already forgiven all men for their sin, but that it remains for humans to accept this forgiveness. "In Jesus, I have forgiven all humans for their sins against me, but only some choose relationship" (225). "When Jesus forgave those who nailed him to the cross they were no longer in his debt, nor mine. In my relationship with those men, I will never bring up what they did, or shame them, or embarrass them" (225). Only when men choose to embrace God's offer of forgiveness will they be redeemed. "[H]e too is my son. I want to redeem him" (224), says God of the man who killed Mack's daughter. Yet the Bible makes it clear that redemption has already been accomplished. The redemption of God's children was accomplished once and for all when Jesus died on the cross. All that awaits now is the application of that redemption to the children of God.

Taken together, Young's muddying of redemption and his incomplete gospel message presents a troubling view of salvation. *The Shack* certainly does not make plain what is made plain in the Bible--that Jesus Christ is the one and the only way to be reconciled to the Father and this only by faith in Him. The book presents less than the full gospel message. It teaches that God died for the sins of the whole world and that He now waits for us to respond to this potential gift. It teaches that God does not punish sin, but that sin is sufficient punishment in itself. It opens the possibility that people can come to God in ways other than a saving faith in Jesus Christ. It obfuscates the doctrine of salvation that the Bible makes so clear and so central. It muddies the very heart of the faith.

Trinity: Who is God?

While Christianity is a faith that encompasses many doctrines that are difficult to understand, there is none so difficult as the doctrine of the Trinity. Neither is there a doctrine that is so foundational to the faith. Though Christians have long acknowledged that we can never know the fullness of this doctrine, there is much we can know and know with confidence. What I share in this section is what has been taught as orthodox through the long history of the church.

Though definitions of the doctrine of the Trinity may very, at its heart must be three statements: God is three persons. Each person is fully God. There is one God. In these statements we affirm that there is one God but three persons who together make up the Godhead. Each member of the Trinity is equal in the divine attributes; each is fully God. The only differences between them are in the ways they relate to one another and the ways they relate to what has been created. There is one "what" but three "who's." That is, there is one God but three persons.

The Trinity is a central concept to *The Shack* and many who are reading and reviewing it are testifying to its power in helping them understand, perhaps for the first time, the true nature of the Trinity. But does *The Shack* teach what the Bible teaches? We will look now at *The Shack's* teaching about the Trinity and will do so under several headings.

PORTRAYING GOD

The emotional power of *The Shack* depends upon a face-to-face encounter between God and man. God the Father is represented as Papa, an African-American woman; Jesus is in the form of a man of Middle-Eastern descent and the Holy Spirit is portrayed as an Asian woman named Sarayu. Yet the Bible is clear that God

VOCABULARY: DOCTRINE

"What the whole Bible teaches us today about some particular topic."

Wayne Grudem

cannot and must not be portrayed in an image. It is impossible to make the creator a part of His creation and the Bible clearly and repeatedly forbids us from even attempting to do this. "God is spirit, and those who worship him must worship in spirit and truth," says Jesus in John 4:24. The third of the Ten Commandments likewise forbids attempting to make any visual portrayal of God. To worship such an image, to acknowledge it as God or even to pretend it is God is to commit the sin of idolatry. It is to worship a creation rather than the Creator. So while Young's portrayal of Jesus may be

> *"I am the best way any human*
> *can relate to Papa or Sarayu.*
> *To see me is to see them."*

based on some fact, his portrayal of the Father and the Holy Spirit in human form is sinful and expressly forbidden within the Bible. It is no small matter. Describing unrighteous people, the Apostle Paul says, "Claiming to be wise, they became fools, and exchanged the glory of the immortal God for images resembling mortal man and birds and animals and creeping things" (Romans 1:22,23). While claiming to be wise, sinful men portrayed God in the image of man. Paul says that the wrath of God is poured out against all who would do such a thing. How then can we support such a portrayal of God in this book?

We have already seen how the Bible places emphasis on mediation. The history of man's relationship to God is a history of mediation. In *The Shack*, though, we find unmediated communication between man and God and this despite the Bible's clear teaching that man cannot approach God without a mediator. "For there is one God, and there is one mediator between God and men, the man Christ Jesus"

SPIRITUAL DISCERNMENT

Spiritual discernment is not a popular subject among Christians today. Yet if we look to the Bible we find that it is a practice that God demands of all who wish to follow Christ. It is a practice or a discipline that the Bible continually relates to spiritual maturity. Those who are mature are those who are discerning; those who are discerning are those who are mature. According to Hebrews 5:14, "solid food is for the mature, for those who have their powers of discernment trained by constant practice to distinguish good from evil." There is a clear relationship between maturity and discernment.

The Bible tells us that discernment is the mark of those who have spiritual life, the mark of those who are experiencing spiritual growth and the mark of those who have attained spiritual maturity. Conversely, the Bible tells us that a lack of discernment is the mark of those who are immature, who are backsliding or who are spiritually dead. God wants His followers to be men and women who practice and who attain to spiritual maturity and spiritual discernment.

What, then, is discernment? It is "the skill of understanding and applying God's Word with the purpose of separating truth from error and right from wrong." Discernment is knowing what God says to us in the Bible so that we can apply this to our lives and live in the way God would have us live. It is a skill that demands practice and one that demands intimate familiarity with the Bible. It is an ability that allows us, with God's help, to filter what is true about God from what is false.

In this booklet we are attempting to exercise spiritual discernment, looking first to the Bible as our guide, as our standard, and comparing *The Shack* to the measure God has given us.

(1 Timothy 2:5). Because we are polluted by sin, we have no right to stand before God without the presence of a mediator. And that mediator must be Jesus Christ, the One who, by His death and resurrection, proved Himself worthy and able. His mediation is the only mediation God will accept. We may boldly approach God as our Father, but only through Jesus Christ (see Hebrews 4:14-16). To suggest we can approach God in an unmediated way is to suggest that we are worthy of approaching God face-to-face despite our sin; it is to suggest that the mediation of Jesus Christ is unnecessary. To do this is to make much of ourselves and to make little of Christ.

ROLES & HIERARCHY

It is critical that we look to the Bible to properly define the roles carried out by each member of the Trinity. When we do this, we see that while the members of the Trinity work together in perfect harmony, each has unique functions. Thus in creation we see that each of the members of the Trinity was active, the Father speaking the words that brought the universe into being, the Son carrying out the work of creation and the Holy Spirit sustaining it or manifesting God's presence over it. The Trinity is active also in redemption, the Father planning redemption and sending His Son as redeemer; the Son being obedient to the Father and accomplishing the work of redemption; the Holy Spirit being sent by the Son in order to apply redemption to God's children.

One thing stands out. In each case we see that the Father is the one who takes the lead. Much as a father relates to a son, the heavenly Father relates to *His* Son. The Father leads and directs and exercises some degree of authority over the Son. The Son is obedient to the directives of the Father and submits to Him. Just as the citizens of a nation are subordinate to the authority of the President, and just as the difference is not in their being or worth but in their role, in the same way, the Son is subordinate to the Father. This is the way it always has been and, according to 1 Corinthians 15:28, the way it always will be. Theologian Bruce Ware says rightly that "the most marked characteristic of the trinitarian relationships is the presence of an eternal and inherent expression of authority and submission." From this we learn that both authority and submission are good, for both are expressive of God himself. And we must then affirm that equality of essence does not conflict with the distinction in roles. The Son may submit to the Father and the Spirit may submit to the Son and the Father, even while maintaining absolute equality in worth and essence.

> *"In Jesus, I have forgiven all humans for their sins against me, but only some choose relationship."*

Such a view is not only lacking in *The Shack*, but is flatly contradicted. While the author affirms the equality of each of the members of the Trinity, he denies that submission can be present in such a relationship. "Mackenzie, we have no concept of final authority among us, only unity. We are in a *circle* of relationship, not a chain of command or 'great chain of being' as your ancestors termed it. What you're seeing here is relationship without any overlay of power. We don't need power over the other because we are always looking out for the best. Hierarchy would make no sense among us" (122). Young goes so far as to suggest that submission is inherently evil—that it is possible only where there is sin. "You humans are so lost and damaged that to you it is almost incomprehensible that relationship could exist apart from hierarchy. So you think that God must relate inside a hierarchy like you do. But we do not" (124). Scripture says otherwise and it says so clearly. "But I want you to understand that the head of every man is Christ, the head of a wife is her husband, and the head of Christ is God" (1 Corinthians 11:3). In John 6:38 Jesus says "I have come down from heaven, not to do my own will but the will of him who sent me" and in 8:28 he makes the astounding claim that "I do nothing on my own authority, but speak just as the Father taught me." This is a Savior who is equal to the Father in essence but subordinate in role. The Father does not obey the Son but the Son obeys the Father. William Young gets these relationships entirely wrong.

Denying roles and hierarchy within the Trinity is an error that has implications that may reach to the very foundations of human relationships. When we properly understand the hierarchy within the Godhead we understand that hierarchy and submission are not products of sin but are present even within the most perfect relationship. This teaches us that we may and must submit in our human relationships and that we can do so without sin. The trinitarian relationship is a model to us of how we honor God by submitting to Him and to the authorities He has seen fit to place over us.

DISTINCTION

While we affirm that there is only one God, we must maintain distinction between the persons of the Trinity. The Father is not the Son, nor is the Son the Father. When we blur these distinctions we wind up with a view of God that begins to lose any sense. Yet it seems that within *The Shack* the distinctions are lost and the persons and roles begin to blend together. Some have suggested that William Young falls into a heresy known as modalism. While I am not convinced that he goes

quite so far, I do find that his view of the Trinity blurs important distinctions. It may be that he does cross the line into modalism and if he does cross such a line, he does so when he maintains that each of the members of the Trinity somehow took on human flesh. Scripture, though, maintains that it was only the Son who did this and only the Son who ever *could* have done this.

In one of his first encounters with Papa, "Mack noticed the scars in her wrists, like those he now assumed Jesus also had on his" (95). Note that these scars were present on the wrists of the Father and not just the Son. Explaining this Papa says, "Don't ever think that what my son chose to do didn't cost us dearly. Love always leaves a significant mark," she stated

"You're talking about the church as this woman you're in love with; I'm pretty sure I haven't met her…She's not the place I go on Sundays."

softly and gently. "We were there *together*" (96).

How could this be that the Father was on the cross? It becomes clear just a few pages later where Papa remarks, "When we three spoke ourself into human existence as the Son of God, we became fully human. We also chose to embrace all the limitations that this entailed. Even though we have always been present in this created universe, we now became flesh and blood" (99). Yet nowhere in Scripture do we find that the Father spoke Himself into human existence; nowhere do we find that the Holy Spirit spoke Himself into human existence. It was only Jesus who became human, even while maintaining His divinity. He is the God-man, God made flesh. We should not say and cannot say, as Mack does to Papa, "I'm so sorry that you, that Jesus, had to die" (103). Jesus died on that cross; the Father did not. We cannot believe that "Papa has crawled inside of your world" (165). We must maintain proper distinctions between the members of the Trinity. Without such distinctions we allow ourselves to believe in a false God—a God other than the One who has revealed Himself in the Bible.

IDENTITY

Young chooses to portray God the Father as feminine, yet with the masculine title Papa. Here is how Papa explains this mystery. "Mackenzie, I am neither male nor female, even though both genders are derived from my nature. If I choose to *appear* to you as a man or a woman, it's because I love you. For me to appear to you as a woman and suggest you call me Papa is simply to mix metaphors, to help you keep from falling so easily back into your religious conditioning" (93). Because

"For almost two days, tied to the big oak at the back of the house, he was beaten with a belt and Bible verses every time his dad woke from a stupor and put down his bottle."

God is Spirit and does not have a body, Young is correct that He is neither male nor female, at least insofar as it relates to anatomy. Clearly God does not and cannot have male or female anatomy. Yet God has chosen to reveal Himself as masculine. Nowhere in the Bible would we find any suggestions that God expects us to relate to Him in anything *but* masculine terms. Nowhere is God known as our Mother. Nor does the Bible give us the leeway to re-imagine God as female—as a Goddess. God has given us revelation of Himself and we re-imagine Him only at our own peril.

Young also teaches a strange view about the very nature of God. He draws upon the name of God as God

revealed Himself to Moses in the familiar words of Exodus 3:14. "God said to Moses, 'I am who I am.' And he said, 'Say this to the people of Israel, 'I am has sent me to you.'" Quoting Buckminster Fuller, a Unitarian-Universalist who wrote a book entitled *I Am a Verb*, he has Papa say, "I am a verb. I am that I am. I will be who I will be. I am a verb! I am alive, dynamic, ever active, and moving. I am verb" (204). Papa explains further saying, "If the universe is only a mass of nouns, it is dead. Unless 'I am,' there are no verbs, and verbs are what makes the universe alive" (204). By implication this would seem to indicate that God is not a person or a being, but a *force*. Verbs are not what make the universe alive; rather, verbs describe the actions of beings that are already alive and active. It is God who makes the universe what it is by being who He is. Though we affirm that God is alive and active in the world, He is no verb. Such a teaching casts doubt on the personhood of God. We can only relate to God as a person, as a noun, and not as a verb.

THE GLORY OF GOD

One of the most disturbing aspects of *The Shack* is the behavior of Mack when he is in the presence of God. When we read in the Bible about those who were given glimpses of God, these people were overwhelmed by His glory. In Isaiah 6 the prophet is allowed to see "the Lord sitting upon a throne, high and lifted up" (Isaiah 6:1). Isaiah reacts by crying out "Woe is me! For I am lost; for I am a man of unclean lips, and I dwell in the midst of a people of unclean lips; for my eyes have seen the King, the Lord of hosts" (Isaiah 6:5)! Isaiah declares a curse upon himself for being a man whose lips are willing to utter unclean words even in a world created by a God of such glory and perfection. When Moses encountered God in the burning bush, he hid his face for he was afraid to look at God's glory (Exodus 3:6). In Exodus 33 Moses is given just a glimpse of God's glory, but God will show only His back saying "you cannot see my face, for man shall not see me and live" (Genesis 33:20). Examples abound. When we look to the Bible's descriptions of heaven we find that any creatures who are in the presence of God are overwhelmed and overjoyed, crying out about God's glory day and night.

But in *The Shack* we find a man who stands in the very presence of God and uses foul language ("damn" (140) and "son of a bitch" (224)), who expresses anger to God (which in turns makes God cry) (92), and who snaps at God in his anger (96). This is not a man who is in the presence of One who is far superior to Him, but a man who is in the presence of a peer. This portrayal of the relationship of man to God and God to man is a far cry from the Bible's portrayal. And indeed it must be because the God of *The Shack* is only a vague resemblance to the God of the Bible. There is no sense of awe as we, through Mack, come into the presence of God.

Gone is the majesty of God when men stand in His holy presence and profane His name. Should God allow in His presence the very sins for which He sent His Son to die? Would a man stand before the Creator of the Universe and curse? What kind of God is the God of *The Shack*?

SUFFERING AND THE GLORY OF GOD

Since time immemorial humans have wrestled with the question of how a good and loving God could allow evil--the kind of evil we see on display all around us in this world and the kind of evil William Young describes in *The Shack*. How do we react to a world where a man can steal and kill a young child? Where is God in the midst of such suffering? And digging deeper still, what possible reason can there be for such suffering? John Piper answers this question in a convincing manner in *Suffering and the Sovereignty of God*. Suffering, he says, exists in order to display the greatness of God.

"The ultimate reason that suffering exists in the universe is so that Christ might display the greatness of the glory of the grace of God by suffering in himself to overcome our suffering. The suffering of the utterly innocent and infinitely holy Son of God in the place of utterly undeserving sinners to bring us to everlasting joy is the greatest display of the glory of God's grace that ever was, or ever could be.

"This was the moment--Good Friday--for which everything in the universe was planned. In conceiving a universe in which to display the glory of his grace, God did not choose Plan B. There could be no greater display of the glory of the Grace of God than what happened at Calvary. Everything leading to it and everything flowing from it is explained by it, including all the suffering in the world."

RECOMMENDED READING

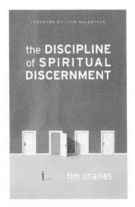
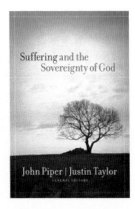
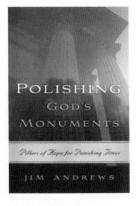
Focusing on just three of the subjects William Young discusses in *The Shack*, we've seen that errors abound. He presents a false view of God and one that may well be described as heretical. He downplays the importance and uniqueness of the Bible, subjugating it or making it equal to other forms of subjective revelation. He misrepresents redemption and salvation, opening the door to the possibility of salvation outside of the completed work of Jesus Christ on the cross. We are left with an unbiblical understanding of the persons and nature of God and of His work in this world.

But this is not all. The discerning reader will note as well that the author muddies the concepts of forgiveness and free will. He introduces teaching that is entirely foreign to the Bible, often stating with certainty what is merely speculative. He oversteps the bounds of Scripture while downplaying the Bible's importance. He relies too little on Scripture and too much on his own theological imaginings.

All this is not to say there is nothing of value in the book. However, it is undeniable to the reader who will look to the Bible, that there is a great deal of error within *The Shack*. There is too much error.

That *The Shack* is a dangerous book should be obvious from this review. The book's subversive undertones seek to dismantle many aspects of the faith and these are subsequently replaced with doctrine that is just plain wrong. Error abounds.

I urge you, the reader, to exercise care in reading and distributing this book. *The Shack* may be an engaging read but it is one that contains far too much error. Read it only with the utmost care and concern, critically evaluating the book against the unchanging standard of Scripture. Caveat lector!

Tim Challies, a self-employed web designer, is a pioneer in the Christian blogosphere, having one of the most widely read and recognized Christian blogs. He is also editor of Discerning Reader, a site dedicated to offering thoughtful reviews of books that are of interest to Christians. He is the author of *The Discipline of Spiritual Discernment*.

tim@challies.com | www.challies.com | www.discerningreader.com

CHALLIES.com
...Informing The Reforming

A LETTER FROM THE PUBLISHER

This is the place traditionally reserved for the colophon, which is defined as follows by Webster's Revised Unabridged, copyright 1996, 1998, MICRA, Inc.:

> \Col"o*phon\ (k[o^]l"[-o]*f[o^]n), n. [L. colophon *finishing stroke,* Gr. kolofw`n; cf. L. culmen top, collis hill. Cf. Holm.] An inscription, monogram, or cipher, containing the place and date of publication, printer's name, etc., formerly placed on the last page of a book.

The current usage of the colophon in the publishing industry is to describe the fonts used in the book. But I think the last page in the book is too important to be devoted to a discussion of its design. So I always like to find a substantive finishing stroke for each book that I publish.

In this case, I think it is only fair to quote from Windblown Media's Wayne Jacobsen's impassioned defense of *The Shack* on their webpage:

> *Our hope was to help people see how the Loving Creator can penetrate our defenses and lead us to healing. Our prayer is that through this book people will see the God of the Bible as Jesus presented him to be—an endearing reality who wants to love us out of our sin and bondage and into his life. This is a message of grace and healing that does not condone or excuse sin, but shows God destroying it through the dynamic relationship he wants with each of his children.*

> *We realize folks will disagree. We planned on it. We appreciate the interaction of those who have honest concerns and questions. Those who have been captured by this story are encouraged to search the Scriptures to see if these things are so and not trust us or the ravings of those who misinterpret this book, either threatened by its success, or those who want to ride on it to push their own fear-based agenda.* [1]

To which I can only say, Amen! By all means, read the Scriptures.

---

[1] http://www.windblownmedia.com/shackresponse.html